To a very good boy called Joseph   G.B.

Text by Sophie Piper
Illustrations copyright © 2008 Georgie Birkett
This edition copyright © 2008 Lion Hudson

The moral rights of the author and illustrator
have been asserted

A Lion Children's Book
an imprint of
Lion Hudson plc
Wilkinson House, Jordan Hill Road,
Oxford OX2 8DR, England
www.lionhudson.com
UK ISBN 978 0 7459 6043 2
US ISBN 978 0 8254 7841 3

First edition 2008
1 3 5 7 9 10 8 6 4 2

Typeset in 34/40 Tapioca ITC
Printed and bound in China

Distributed by:
UK: Marston Book Services Ltd, PO Box 269, Abingdon, Oxon OX14 4YN
USA: Trafalgar Square Publishing, 814 N Franklin Street, Chicago, IL 60610
USA Christian Market: Kregel Publications, PO Box 2607, Grand Rapids, MI 49501

How to be Good

Sophie Piper
Georgie Birkett

LION
CHILDREN'S

Clean is clean

and grubby is...

Oh dear!

But is clean good?

It can be.

Tidy is tidy

and untidy is... Oh dear!

Oops

But is tidy good?
It can be.

Quiet is quiet

and dreamy and peaceful.

But is quiet good?

It can be.

It sort of depends on the noise...

la la la

boom bash crash

It sort of depends on the quiet...

tip toe, tip toe

Kind is good...

and so is gentle.

Helpful is good, even if...

Oops

it doesn't always work out.

Truthful is good...

Sorry

and so is putting things right.

Thinking of others is good.

Happy birthday

Come and play

It is good to laugh with those who are happy.

When someone is sad,

it is good to comfort them.

Caring is good...

and so is sharing...

and loving is best of all.